COLONIAL AMERICA HISTORY

FOR KIDS

BY: JAMES BREZNICKY

We the People of the United States, in Order to form a more perfect Union, establish Justice, insure domestic Tranquility, provide for the common defence, promote the general Welfare, and secure the Blessings of Liberty to ourselves and our Posterity, do ordain and establish this Constitution for the United States of America.
Article. I.
Section. 1. All legislative Powers herein granted shall be vested in a Congress of the United States, which shall consist of a Senate and House of Representatives.

Hi do you live in the U.S.A?
And wonder about it's history as you play.
The people who settled on this land.
Had a mighty fine plan.

It started with the Declaration of Independence which was signed in July.
All because tension with British was high.
The British Empire was being very cruel.
That is why the Americans left their rule.

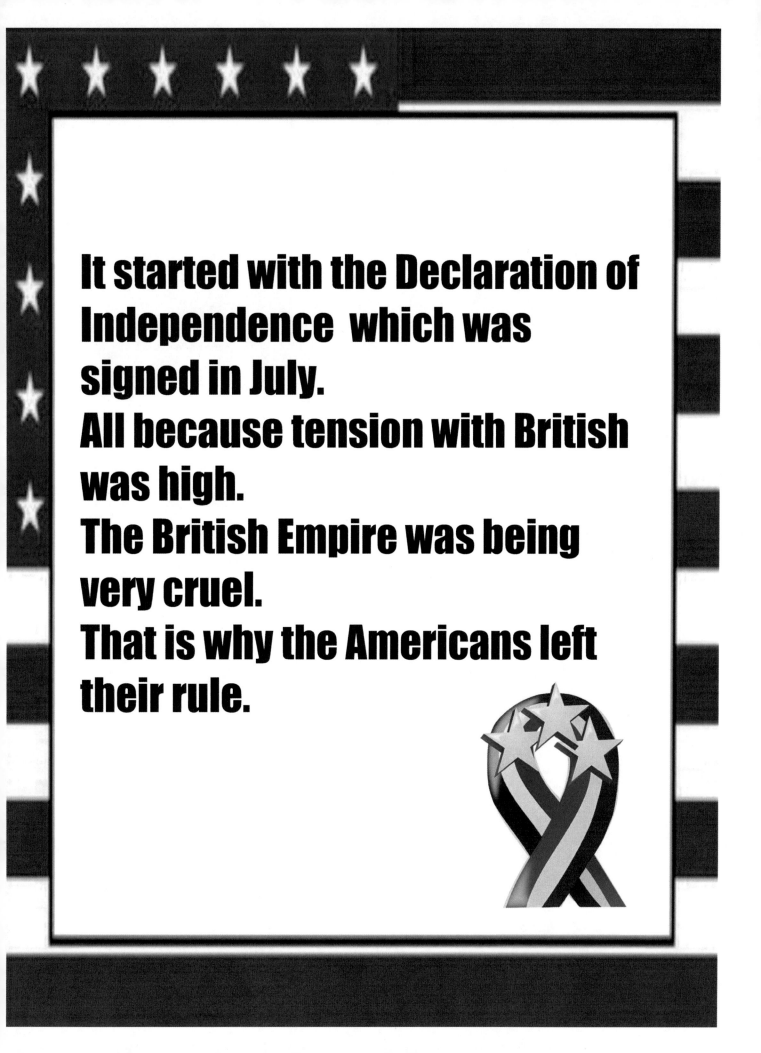

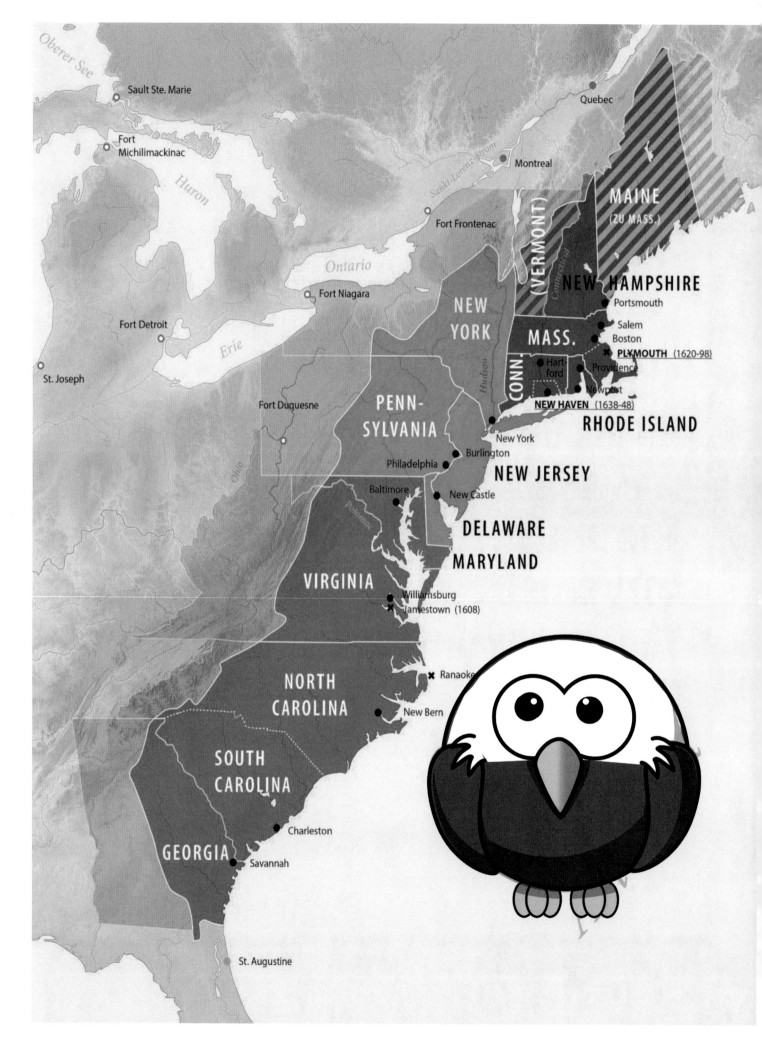

Originally there was thirteen states.
And a revolutionary war would decide their fate.
But now we are 50 states strong.
With this union we can't go wrong.

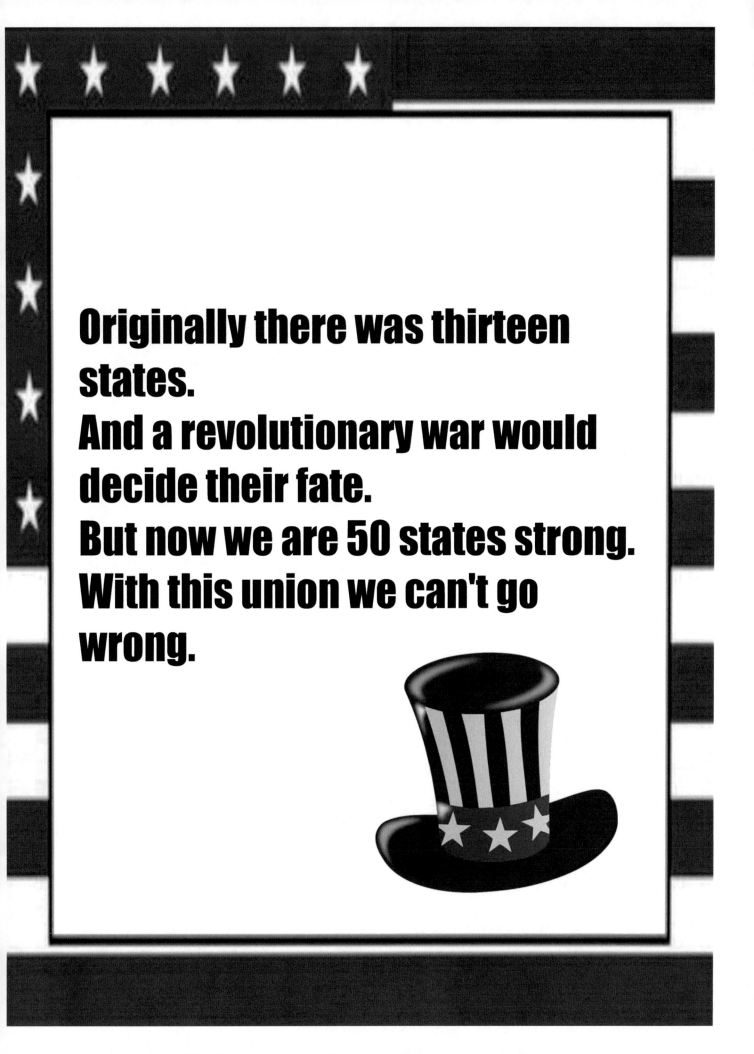

First they had to make a law of the land.
So the Constitution fit that plan.
It outlined the type of government the people desired.
After they wrote it i'm sure they were tired.

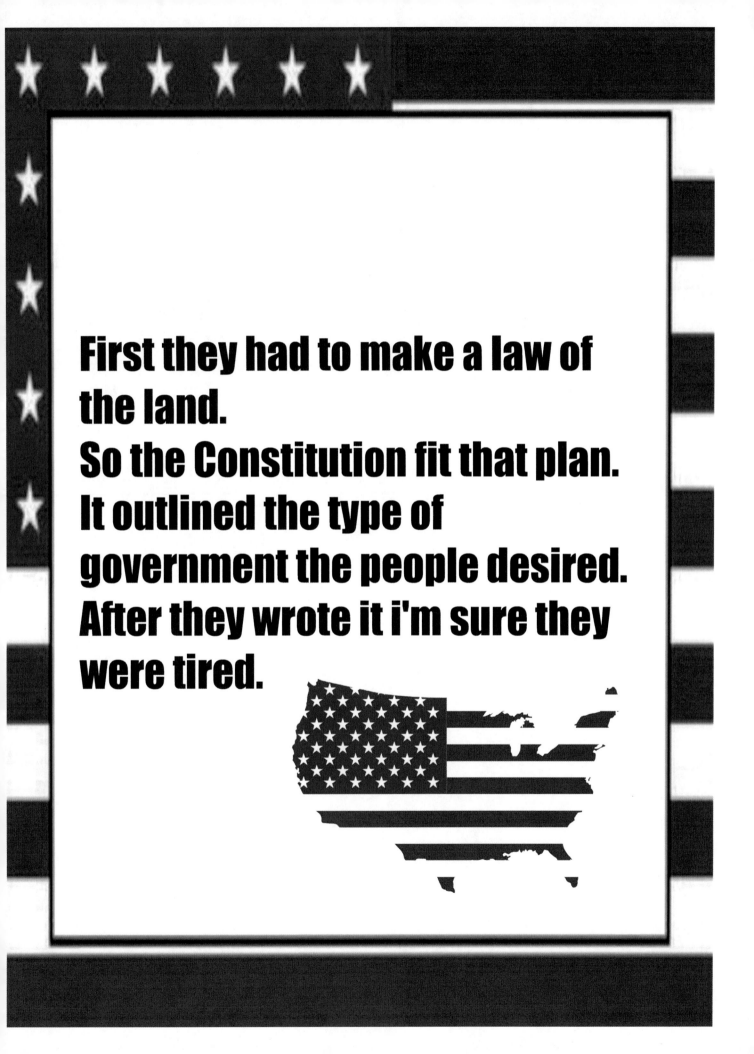

We the People

of the United States, in order to... insure domestic Tranquility, provide for the common defence, promote the general Welfare, and secure the Blessings of Liberty to ourselves and our Posterity, do ordain and establish this Constitution for the United States of America.

Article. 1.

Section. 1. All legislative Powers herein granted shall be vested in a Congress of the United States, which shall consist of a Senate and House of Representatives.

Section. 2. The House of Representatives shall be composed of Members chosen every second Year by the People of the several States, and the Electors in each State shall have the Qualifications requisite for Electors of the most numerous Branch of the State Legislature.

No Person shall be a Representative who shall not have attained to the Age of twenty five Years, and been seven Years a Citizen of the United States, and who shall not, when elected, be an Inhabitant of that State in which he shall be chosen.

Representatives and direct Taxes shall be apportioned among the several States which may be included within this Union, according to their respective Numbers, which shall be determined by adding to the whole Number of free Persons, including those bound to Service for a Term of Years, and excluding Indians not taxed, three fifths of all other Persons. The actual Enumeration shall be made within three Years after the first Meeting of the Congress of the United States, and within every subsequent Term of ten Years, in such Manner as they shall by Law direct. The Number of Representatives shall not exceed one for every thirty Thousand, but each State shall have at Least one Representative; and until such enumeration shall be made, the State of New Hampshire shall be entitled to chuse three, Massachusetts eight, Rhode-Island and Providence Plantations one, Connecticut five, New-York six, New Jersey four, Pennsylvania eight, Delaware one, Maryland six, Virginia ten, North Carolina five, South Carolina five, and Georgia three.

When vacancies happen in the Representation from any State, the Executive Authority thereof shall issue Writs of Election to fill such Vacancies.

The House of Representatives shall chuse their Speaker and other Officers; and shall have the sole Power of Impeachment.

Section. 3. The Senate of the United States shall be composed of two Senators from each State, chosen by the Legislature thereof, for six Years; and each Senator shall have one Vote.

Immediately after they shall be assembled in Consequence of the first Election, they shall be divided as equally as may be into three Classes. The Seats of the Senators of the first Class shall be vacated at the Expiration of the second Year, of the second Class at the Expiration of the fourth Year, and of the third Class at the Expiration of the sixth Year, so that one third may be chosen every second Year; and if Vacancies happen by Resignation, or otherwise, during the Recess of the Legislature of any State, the Executive thereof may make temporary Appointments until the next Meeting of the Legislature, which shall then fill such Vacancies.

No Person shall be a Senator who shall not have attained to the Age of thirty Years, and been nine Years a Citizen of the United States, and who shall not, when elected, be an Inhabitant of that State for which he shall be chosen.

The Vice President of the United States shall be President of the Senate, but shall have no Vote, unless they be equally divided.

The Senate shall chuse their other Officers, and also a President pro tempore, in the Absence of the Vice President, or when he shall exercise the Office of President of the United States.

The Senate shall have the sole Power to try all Impeachments. When sitting for that Purpose, they shall be on Oath or Affirmation. When the President of the United States is tried, the Chief Justice shall preside: And no Person shall be convicted without the Concurrence of two thirds of the Members present.

Judgment in Cases of Impeachment shall not extend further than to removal from Office, and disqualification to hold and enjoy any Office of honor, Trust or Profit under the United States: but the Party convicted shall nevertheless be liable and subject to Indictment, Trial, Judgment and Punishment, according to Law.

Section. 4. The Times, Places and Manner of holding Elections for Senators and Representatives, shall be prescribed in each State by the Legislature thereof; but the Congress may at any time by Law make or alter such Regulations, except as to the Places of chusing Senators.

The Congress shall assemble at least once in every Year, and such Meeting shall be on the first Monday in December, unless they shall by Law appoint a different Day.

Section. 5. Each House shall be the Judge of the Elections, Returns and Qualifications of its own Members, and a Majority of each shall constitute a Quorum to do Business; but a smaller Number may adjourn from day to day, and may be authorized to compel the Attendance of absent Members, in such Manner, and under such Penalties as each House may provide.

Each House may determine the Rules of its Proceedings, punish its Members for disorderly Behaviour, and, with the Concurrence of two thirds, expel a Member.

Each House shall keep a Journal of its Proceedings, and from time to time publish the same, excepting such Parts as may in their Judgment require Secrecy; and the Yeas and Nays of the Members of either House on any question shall, at the Desire of one fifth of those Present, be entered on the Journal.

Neither House, during the Session of Congress, shall, without the Consent of the other, adjourn for more than three days, nor to any other Place than that in which the two Houses shall be sitting.

Section. 6. The Senators and Representatives shall receive a Compensation for their Services, to be ascertained by Law, and paid out of the Treasury of the United States. They shall in all Cases, except Treason, Felony and Breach of the Peace, be privileged from Arrest during their Attendance at the Session of their respective Houses, and in going to and returning from the same; and for any Speech or Debate in either House, they shall not be questioned in any other Place.

No Senator or Representative shall, during the Time for which he was elected, be appointed to any civil Office under the Authority of the United States, which shall have been created, or the Emoluments whereof shall have been increased during such time; and no Person holding any Office under the United States, shall be a Member of either House during his Continuance in Office.

Section. 7. All Bills for raising Revenue shall originate in the House of Representatives; but the Senate may propose or concur with Amendments as on other Bills.

Every Bill which shall have passed the House of Representatives and the Senate, shall, before it become a Law, be presented to the President of the...

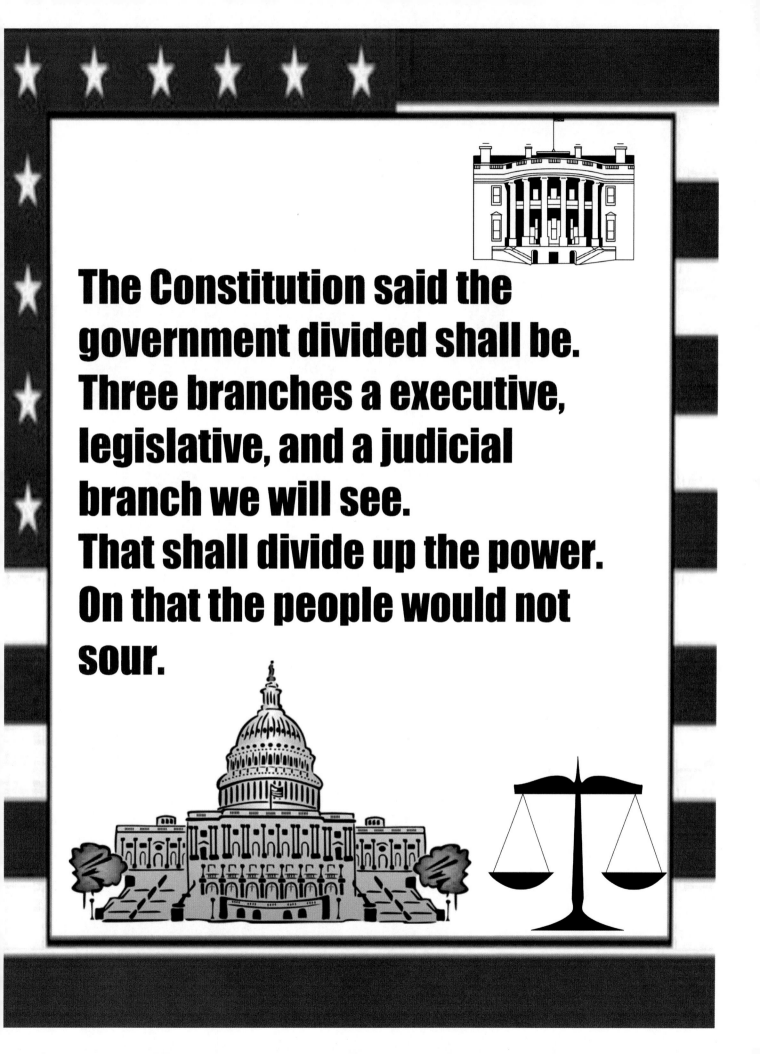

The Constitution said the government divided shall be.
Three branches a executive, legislative, and a judicial branch we will see.
That shall divide up the power.
On that the people would not sour.

George Washington was President number one.
I am sure at the time it was not fun.
I bet his time was spent planning.
And for the British he had to keep scanning.

The U.S.A. needed a flag.
One that the people could brag.
For that task Betsy Ross did they turn.
Her place in history she did earn.

The stars on the flag would represent each state.
For that would be its fate.
And the the original colonies are represented by stripes of thirteen.
Red, white, and blue color gives the flag a nice sheen.

And did you know the flag has its own holiday?
With a flag so beautiful that is totally ok.
June fourteenth would be the day its true.
It is the day we honor the red, white, and blue.

Benjamin Franklin is who we will talk about next.

Being the first Postmaster General and a Ambassador to France was some of his biggest flex.

He was also a scientist and inventor and spent a lot of time writing.

Benjamin even did a experiment on electricity by flying a kite with a key on it to get struck by lighting.

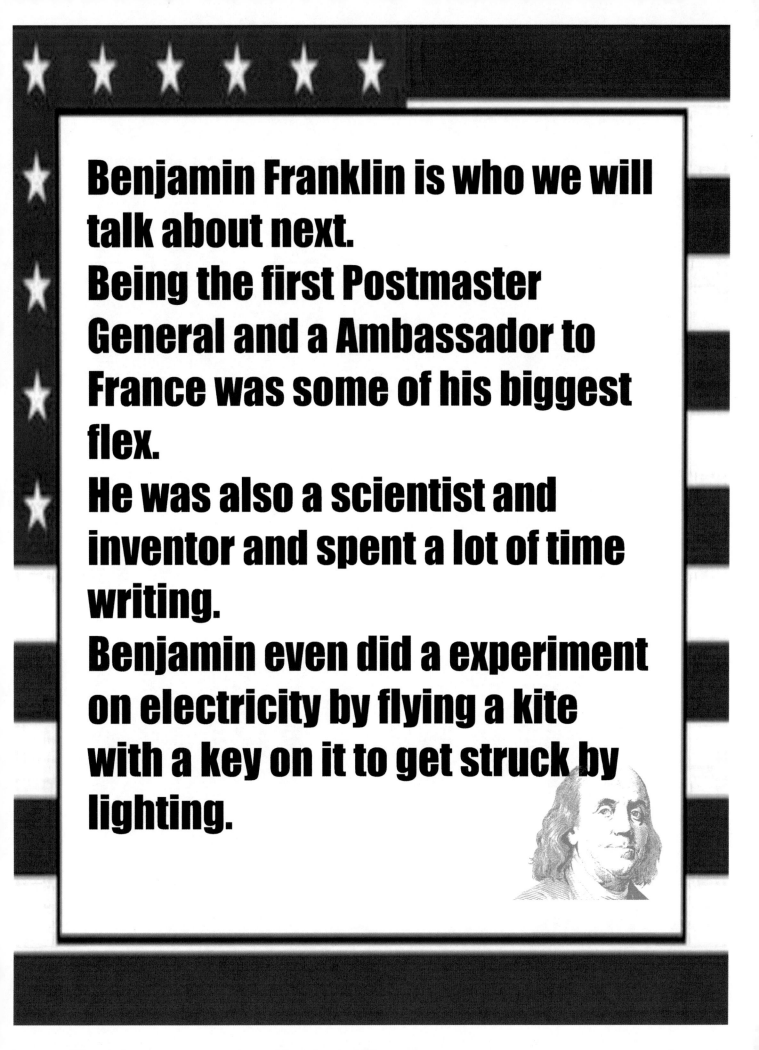

The next founder is John Hancock
When it came to freedom he did not balk.
Signing the Declaration of Independence and becoming Massachusetts Governor was some of his first.
His quest for freedom was his biggest thirst.

John Hancock

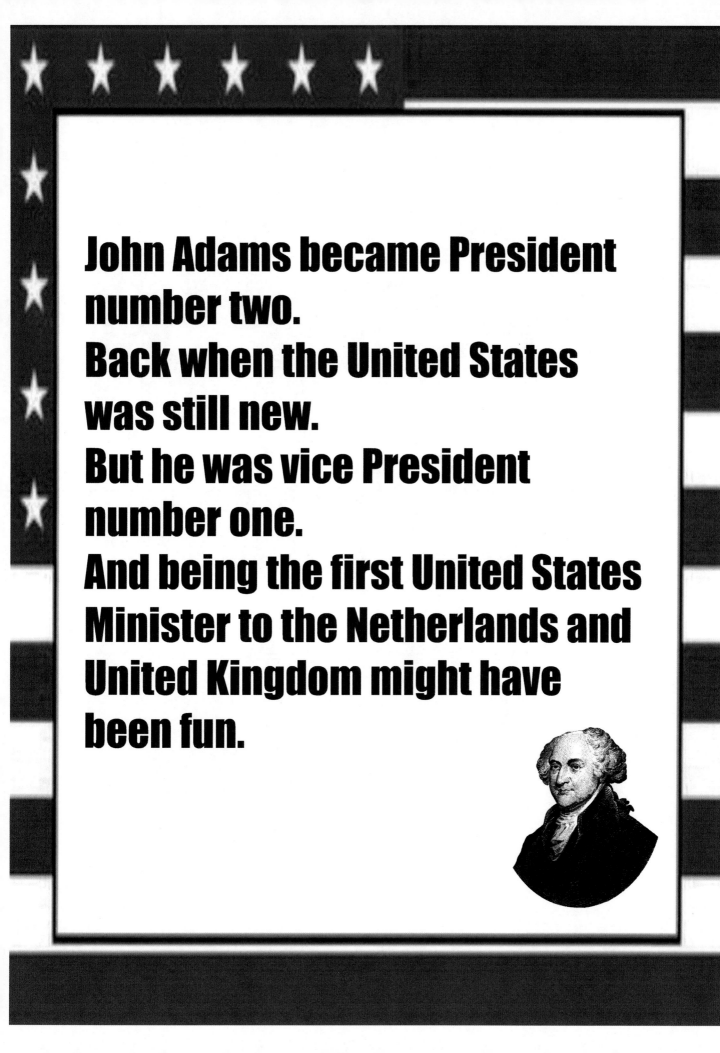

John Adams became President number two.
Back when the United States was still new.
But he was vice President number one.
And being the first United States Minister to the Netherlands and United Kingdom might have been fun.

Next I will tell you about the liberty bell.
In Pennsylvania is where it will dwell.
It has a really big crack.
They say after a Chief Justice died someone gave it a big whack.

The United States of America declared its independence on July fourth.

So that makes it the U.S.A. birthday and it is celebrated from east, west, south, and north.

On this day most people watch fireworks and go to parties where they eat.

And now you know some of the U.S.A founding history I will leave you until next time we meet.

Made in the USA
Las Vegas, NV
02 December 2023

81963773R00019